WHERE'S CHURCHILL?

A STUDIO PRESS BOOK

First published in the UK in 2020 by Studio Press,
an imprint of Bonnier Books UK,
The Plaza, 535 King's Road, London SW10 0SZ
Owned by Bonnier Books
Sveavägen 56, Stockholm, Sweden

www.studiopressbooks.co.uk
www.bonnierbooks.co.uk

1 3 5 7 9 10 8 6 4 2

ISBN 978-1-78741-845-5

Concept and text by Ryan Gearing
Illustrations by Daniel McCloskey
Edited by Stephanie Milton and Sophia Akhtar
Designed by Rob Ward
Production by Emma Kidd

A CIP catalogue for this book is available from the British Library

Printed and bound in Spain

WHERE'S CHURCHILL?

A WORLD WAR TWO
SEARCH & FIND BOOK

WHO TO FIND

Winston Churchill

Winston Churchill was a British statesman, orator and author who was Prime Minister during the Second World War. As an inspirational leader in this time of war, he made stirring speeches to encourage the fight against Hitler and the Axis powers. He led his country from the brink of defeat to victory.

Churchill is hiding in every location, supported by some of his closest allies. But Britain's wartime leader has also been spotted by Axis forces, so beware – you'll spot his enemies in every scene, as well as his friends.

Otto Kretschmer

The most successful submarine commander of any navy during the Second World War. In the first 18 months of the war he sank 47 ships, totalling over 266,000 tons. His reward was celebrity status in Nazi Germany.

Karl Dönitz

Chosen to create the German U-boat fleet. Under his guidance, the U-boats operated in 'wolfpack' formation, patrolling in long lines and joining in their attacks to overwhelm the convoy by weight of numbers.

Max Horton

Horton played a key role in the Battle of the Atlantic, developing aggressive tactics for the Royal Navy to take the fight to the U-boats and ensuring shipping lanes stayed open to provide Britain with vital arms and supplies.

Ernst Lindemann

Commander of the German battleship *Bismarck*, the pride of the Kriegsmarine (Nazi Germany's navy). At the time, this was the largest warship in commission anywhere in the world at over 280ft and armed with eight 15" naval guns, each with a range of over 20 miles.

Frederick Bowhill

In charge of the RAF's Coastal Command. He used his knowledge of the sea (gained from experience during the First World War) to identify the position of the German battleship *Bismarck* using an RAF Catalina flying boat.

Adolf Hitler

The leader of Germany's Nazi Party and one of the most notorious dictators of the 20th century. Hitler exploited economic woes, popular discontent and political infighting to take power in Germany and almost single-handedly brought the world to the very brink of destruction.

Douglas Bader

A legend due to his dogged determination and willpower. He lost both of his legs following a plane crash in 1931 and refused to let this prevent him from re-joining the RAF and flying Spitfires during the Second World War.

Charles de Gaulle

General and statesman who refused to accept the French government's truce with the Germans and escaped to London. Here, de Gaulle established a separate government in exile known as Free France and organised the French Resistance.

Hugh Dowding

Led RAF Fighter Command to victory during the Battle of Britain. He strongly argued that Fighter Command's role was to protect Britain, and he challenged the use of the RAF's resources to protect France.

Hermann Göring

One of Germany's leading Nazi Party leaders, president of the Reichstag and Hitler's designated successor. He was responsible for setting up the Gestapo secret police. Appointed Commissioner for Aviation and head of the Luftwaffe (the German air force).

Neville Chamberlain

British Prime Minister at the outbreak of the Second World War, replaced by Winston Churchill in 1940, when he was forced to resign over a disastrous military campaign in Norway.

Lord Haw-Haw (William Joyce)

A notorious broadcaster of Nazi propaganda to the British during the war. His famous announcement of 'Germany calling, Germany calling' introduced threats and misinformation broadcast by radio from his home in Hamburg to the United Kingdom and United States.

Clement Attlee

Leader of the opposition Labour Party in Britain. He was appointed to the War Cabinet by Churchill in the new coalition Government. Attlee became Deputy Prime Minister, responsible for the day-to-day business on the home front.

King George VI

The royals embraced rationing and made morale-boosting visits to munitions factories and army barracks to support the home front. The King and Queen remained at Buckingham Palace throughout the war, despite nine direct hits.

Mary Churchill

Mary was the youngest child of Winston and Clementine Churchill. During the war, she served with the Red Cross, the Women's Voluntary Service and Auxiliary Territorial Service, in which she served in an anti-aircraft battery.

William Tennant

Beachmaster at Dunkirk responsible for organising the evacuation of more than 300,000 tired and dispirited troops. He was also the last to return to Dover, patrolling the coastline and calling out to see if there were any soldiers still ashore.

Bertram Ramsay

The mastermind of Dunkirk. He formed the plans for the Royal Navy to lead a massive seaborne rescue of the troops in danger of being encircled and captured by the Germans. This was officially called Operation Dynamo.

Franklin D. Roosevelt

The 32nd President of the United States and the only President elected four times. He led the United States to victory over Nazi Germany and helped lay the groundwork for the post-war peace organisation that would become the United Nations.

Isoroku Yamamoto

He devised the attacks against key US military installations in the Pacific Ocean, adding Pearl Harbor at the last minute. As the attacks commenced, the United States formally became part of the Second World War.

Emperor Hirohito

Japan's longest-reigning emperor, holding the throne from 1926 to 1989. He was said to be unenthusiastic about the war but was often pictured in uniform to show support. After surrender in 1945, he became a figurehead only.

Raymond A. Spruance

Often quoted as being one of the greatest admirals in American naval history. He commanded two of the most significant naval battles in the Pacific Theatre: the Battle of Midway and the Battle of the Philippine Sea.

Chester W. Nimitz

Nimitz was promoted to Commander in Chief of the US Pacific Fleet in 1941. In September 1945, he received the formal surrender of Japanese forces on board the battleship USS *Missouri* in Tokyo Bay.

Doris Miller

The first African-American to be awarded the Navy Cross for his actions in rescuing the injured and manning a machine gun, despite having no weapons training, on USS *West Virginia* after it was attacked by the Japanese at Pearl Harbor.

Joseph Stalin

Supreme ruler of the Soviet Union for a quarter of a century. Stalin became Soviet dictator after the death of Lenin in 1924. When Hitler invaded Russia in 1941 and rolled on towards Moscow, Stalin refused to leave, deciding victory must be won at any cost.

WHO TO FIND

Georgi Zhukov

The most acclaimed Soviet military commander of the Second World War. In 1942, Stalin appointed Zhukov Deputy Commander-in-chief of the Red Army and he oversaw the encirclement and surrender of the German Sixth Army.

Vasily Chuikov

Led the forces in the defence of Stalingrad. He is credited as saying 'We shall hold the city or die there'. Much of the fighting, which raged for five months, was at close quarters, hand to hand with bayonets and hand grenades.

Erich von Manstein

One of the most important German officers during the invasion of Russia. He made a significant advance, taking over 430,000 Russian prisoners as he conquered all of Crimea with the capture of the Black Sea port of Sevastopol.

Erwin Rommel

German Army officer renowned as an innovator of armoured tactics with spectacular victories as commander of the Afrika Korps in North Africa. He earned the nickname 'Desert Fox' as he was a wily and aggressive commander.

Tania Chernova

It was not just the men who fought as snipers at Stalingrad. Hundreds of female snipers were trained to fight within the Red Army, and were taught how to aim and fire a rifle. One notable example is Tania Chernova.

Charles Upham, VC & Bar

New Zealand's most famous soldier. One of only three people ever to win the Victoria Cross twice for his actions; Crete in 1941 and Egypt in 1942, where he was captured. As a POW, he made so many attempts to escape that he was finally interned at Colditz Castle for the remainder of the war.

Bernard Montgomery

The most well-known British general of the war. 'Monty' inspired a dispirited and defeated force to claim victory over the Germans and Italians at the Battle of El Alamein. He went on to command the Allies in the invasions of Italy and Normandy.

Giorgio Masina

One of the Italian generals commanding under the German Panzer Army Africa. He took part in all of the major battles of the Western Desert Campaign until captured during the Second Battle of El Alamein.

Claude Auchinleck

Commander-in-chief of the Allied forces in the Middle East in 1941. He saw initial success, but Rommel's German forces picked up momentum in the desert and, with the British Army pushed back to El Alamein, this led to Churchill's decision to replace him with Montgomery.

Nikolai Vatutin

During the Battle of Kursk, the ingenious Russian general buried his tanks so that only the top showed. This was intended to draw the German tanks closer, eliminate the German advantage of long-range fighting and protect Soviet tanks from destruction.

Hermann Hoth

Fought in the Battle of France and as a Panzer commander on the Eastern Front. Hoth had commands during Stalingrad, Kursk and Kiev. He was convicted of war crimes at the Nuremberg Trials after the war and sentenced to 15 years in prison.

Harold Alexander

Wounded twice during the First World War, Alexander won the Military Cross twice. He was the Supreme Allied Commander in Italy, ordering the Cassino offensive combined with an amphibious operation at Anzio.

Mark W. Clark
The youngest four-star-general in the history of the US Army. General Clark led the capture of Rome in 1944 and had a military career spanning both World Wars as well as the Korean War.

Benito Mussolini
Mussolini formed the Fascist Party in 1919 with support from many unemployed First World War veterans. He allied Italy with Nazi Germany and Japan and remained a dictator for 21 years until his arrest and execution in 1945.

Albert Kesselring
One of Hitler's top strategists during the war. It was his defensive action as Commander-in-chief, South, that prevented Allied victory in Italy for more than a year. He was taken prisoner on 6 May 1945 as the Allies approached final victory.

George S. Patton
Led the US Third Army in a successful sweep across France in 1944. His strict discipline, toughness and self-sacrifice elicited pride within his ranks, and the general was colourfully referred to as 'Old Blood-and-Guts' by his men.

Dwight D. Eisenhower
Appointed the Supreme Commander of Allied forces in Europe. On 6 June 1944, he gambled on a break in bad weather and gave the order to launch the Normandy Invasion, the largest amphibious attack in history with the simple words 'OK, let's go'.

Stanisław Sosabowski
Major-General Sosabowski commanded the Polish 1st Independent Parachute Brigade during the Battle of Arnhem, Operation Market Garden. He was portrayed in the Richard Attenborough film *A Bridge Too Far* by Gene Hackman.

Allison Digby Tatham-Warter
Immortalised in the epic 1977 film *A Bridge Too Far.* Digby stated he carried an umbrella because he could never remember passwords and thought it would help identify him as an Englishman at all times.

George Marshall
Marshall served as the US Army Chief of Staff during the war, appointed by Roosevelt on 1 September 1939. He oversaw the expansion of the American forces from a pre-war strength of under 200,000 to one of over eight million at its wartime peak.

Walter Model
Model was one of Hitler's favourite generals. On more than one occasion he prevented a defeat on the Eastern front and was in also in command of the German troops who made short work of British paratroopers during the Battle of Arnhem.

Airey Neave
The first British officer to escape from Colditz, Neave went on to become a Member of Parliament. He crawled through a hole in a camp theatre, after a prisoner performance, to a guardhouse, then boldly marched out dressed as a German soldier.

Harold Henry Schultz
A member of the patrol that captured the top of Mount Suribachi and raised the first US flag on 23 February 1945. He was also one of the six Marines who raised the larger replacement flag on the mountaintop the same day, as seen in the iconic photograph from Iwo Jima.

Leslie (Bill) Goldfinch
One of the soldiers that engineered the most ingenious escape plan never to be put to the test. Bill was one of the team who built the Colditz Cock, a wooden glider built in the lower attic of the castle chapel.

Max Schmidt
The first Kommandant (Oberst) of Colditz, followed by Oberst Glaesche and then Oberst Prawitt. He retired on 31 July 1942 when he was 70. He was arrested by the Russian Secret Police at the end of the war and is reported to have died in hospital in Latvia.

Violette Szabo
Trained as a field agent to work alongside the French Resistance, Violette was captured days after the D-Day landings and later killed. Her life as a British secret agent was immortalised in the Second World War film *Carve Her Name with Pride.*

BATTLE OF THE ATLANTIC (3ʳᵈ SEP 1939 – 8ᵀʰ MAY 1945)

The Battle of the Atlantic was the longest continuous campaign of the entire war. The North Atlantic was the essential lifeline for Britain and the Allies. Cargo ships carried food, oil, tanks, planes, clothes, troops and more.

Convoys grouped merchant ships together, escorted by naval vessels so they could be protected, but they were always subject to German submarines hunting in 'wolf packs'.

Otto Kretschmer

Max Horton

Karl Dönitz

Frederick Bowhill

Ernst Lindemann

COLDITZ CASTLE (1939 – 1945)

Colditz Castle was a German prisoner-of-war camp and the site of many daring escape attempts by Allied officers. It housed high-profile prisoners of many nationalities who had repeatedly escaped from other camps or otherwise given the Germans trouble.

Colditz, official name Oflag IV-C, has been immortalised frequently in fiction, including books, films and television.

Douglas Bader

Colonel Airey Neave

Adolf Hitler

Max Schmidt

Leslie (Bill) Goldfinch

HALT!

DUNKIRK EVACUATION (26TH MAY – 4TH JUN 1940)

The 'miracle of Dunkirk' saw the evacuation of 340,000 British, French, Belgian and Dutch forces at the beaches of Northern France by some 900 vessels, including fishing boats, pleasure boats and ferries, as the Germans closed their grip on the continent.

On the eve of Operation Dynamo, King George VI declared a National Day of Prayer, in which he himself attended a special service at Westminster Abbey.

King George VI **Bertram Ramsay** **William Tennant** **Herman Göring** **Adolf Hitler**

BATTLE OF BRITAIN (10TH JUL – 31ST OCT 1940)

The Battle of Britain, which took place from 10th July until 31st October 1940, thwarted the German Luftwaffe's attempts to gain air supremacy over southern England, averting possible invasion and downing 1,733 German aircraft.

Described by Prime Minister Winston Churchill as the RAF's finest hour, nearly 3,000 men of the RAF took part in the first major military campaign in history to be fought entirely in the air.

Douglas Bader

Hugh Dowding

Charles de Gaulle

Adolf Hitler

Hermann Göring

THE BLITZ (SEP 1940 – MAY 1941)

This was a huge bombing campaign, targeting London and other major cities and carried out by the German air force from September 1940 to May 1941. It was designed to cause devastation and lower the morale of the British people.

Families were forced to sleep underground and in shelters, with many losing their homes. Around 60,000 people were killed and 2 million houses damaged

Neville Chamberlain Clement Attlee Lord Haw-Haw (William Joyce) Mary Churchill Adolf Hitler

ATTACK ON PEARL HARBOR (7TH DEC 1941)

This was a surprise attack by the Japanese on US naval forces on Oahu Island, Hawaii.

On 7 December 1941, waves of dive bombers, torpedo planes and fighters descended, capsizing, destroying or immobilising several US battleships within the first 30 minutes of the raid. The attack resulted in the destruction of 180 US aircraft and more than 3,400 American casualties.

Isoroku Yamamoto

Franklin D. Roosevelt

Raymond A. Spurance

Emperor Hirohito

Doris Miller

HOGA

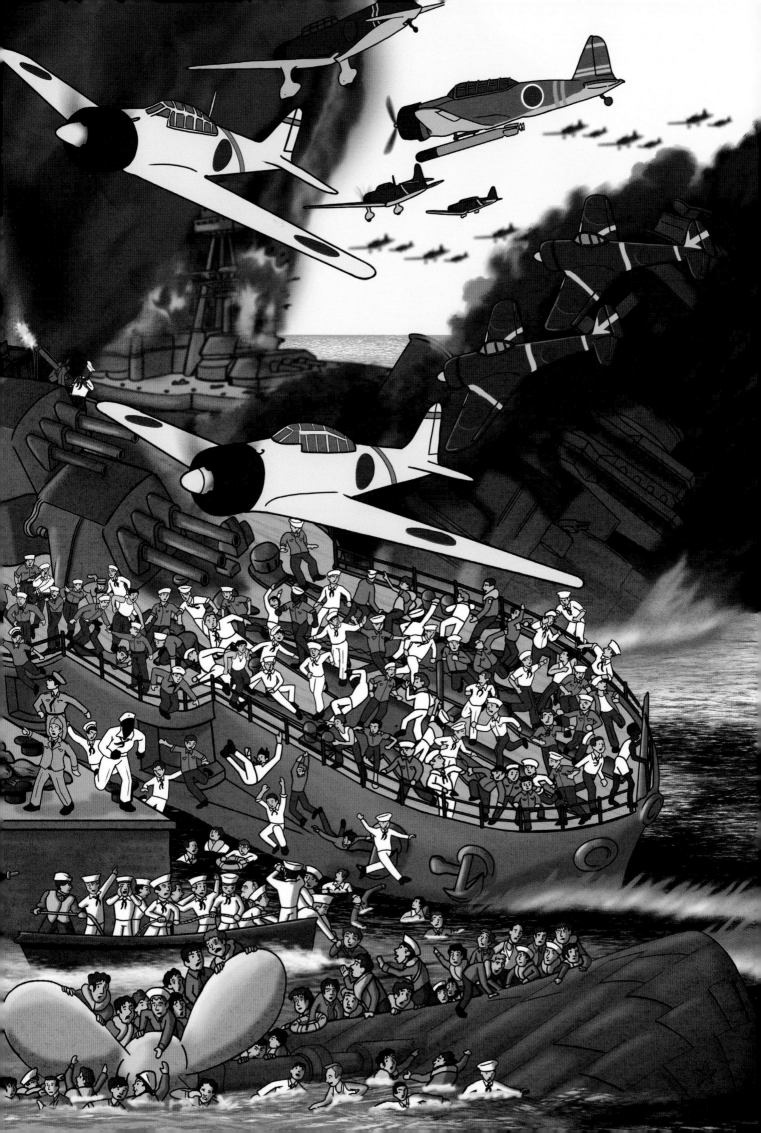

BATTLE OF MIDWAY (4ᵀᴴ – 7ᵀᴴ JUN 1942)

Regarded as the most important battle of the Pacific Campaign. Japan wanted Midway as a base to attack and secure Pearl Harbor and achieve dominance in the region.

American forces were waiting, ambushed and sank the Imperial Japanese Navy's carrier fleet that had previously attacked Pearl Harbor, destroying four aircraft carriers and 250 aircraft.

Franklin D. Roosevelt

Chester Nimitz

Isoroku Yamamoto

Emperor Hirohito

Raymond A. Spurance

BATTLE OF STALINGRAD (23RD AUG 1942 – 2ND FEB 1943)

Throughout 1942 the Germans advanced into Russia as part of Operation Barbarossa until they reached Stalingrad. Here they were brought to a standstill, locked in battle for five months. They fought the Soviets in the streets until, exhausted and running out of supplies, the Germans were surrounded and forced to surrender.

Over 90,000 German soldiers were captured and many then died in prison camps later in the war.

Joseph Stalin

Georgi Zhukov

Erich von Manstein

Vasily Chuikov

Tania Chernova

BATTLE OF EL ALAMEIN (23ʳᴰ OCT – 11ᵀᴴ NOV 1942)

General Auchinleck halted Rommel's Afrika Korps who were heading for Egypt, but Churchill wanted a definitive victory for the British people. He sent a new general, Montgomery, who achieved decisive victory in the Second Battle of El Alamein.

Monty assembled more than 1,000 tanks, 1,500 aircraft and hundreds of guns to begin this battle. By comparison, Rommel was down to around 200 tanks, many of which were in need of repair.

Erwin Rommel

Bernard Montgomery

Charles Upham, VC & Bar

Claude Auchinleck

Giorgio Masina

BATTLE OF KURSK (5TH JUL – 23RD AUG 1943)

Operation Citadel, launched on July 5th 1943, followed the disastrous defeat of the Germans at Stalingrad. The last chance to regain dominance on the Eastern Front, the Battle of Kursk lasted more than a month and involved over 9,000 tanks, 4,000 aircraft and 3 million soldiers. The German effort advanced for four days before meeting Russian resistance and counterattack. Citadel was then cancelled as the Allies landed in Sicily.

Erich von Manstein

Adolf Hitler

Georgy Zhukov

Hermann Hoth

Nikolai Vatutin

BATTLE OF MONTE CASSINO (17TH JAN – 18TH MAY 1944)

This was a series of four assaults involving British, New Zealand, Indian, Polish, French and American forces. It was one of the bloodiest battles against the German defensive line in Italy, lasting some five months.

With close combat fighting amongst the rubble of the monastery ruins, troops encountered some of the worst fighting since the First World War.

Harold Alexander

Mark Clark

Adolf Hitler

Kesselring

Benito Mussolini

INVASION OF NORMANDY (D-DAY) (6ᵀᴴ JUNE 1944)

D-Day marked the start of the Allied landings in Normandy in France during the Second World War. Over 2 million troops from over 12 countries were in Britain, in preparation for the invasion.

On 6ᵗʰ June 1944, around 156,000 American, British and Canadian troops landed on five beaches codenamed Utah, Omaha, Gold, Juno and Sword. More than 13,000 aircraft and 5,000 ships supported the operation.

Dwight D. Eisenhower

Adolf Hitler

Bernard Montgomery

George S. Patton

Violette Szabo

OPERATION MARKET GARDEN (17TH – 25TH SEP 1944)

The goal of Operation Market Garden was to secure the key bridges over three wide rivers in the Netherlands – Meuse, Waal and Rhine – in order to outflank the heavy German defences of the Siegfried Line which protected heartland Germany beyond.

It was hoped that with a swift advance towards Berlin, the war would be over before Christmas.

Bernard Montgomery

'Digby' Tatham-Warter

Dwight D. Eisenhower

Adolf Hitler

Stanislaw Sosabowski

BATTLE OF THE BULGE (16TH DEC 1944 – 25TH JAN 1945)

In December 1944, with the onset of winter, the German Army launched a counteroffensive that was intended to turn the tide in Hitler's favour.

The battle that ensued in the Ardenne Forest is known as the Battle of the Bulge. It was ultimately an unsuccessful attempt to push the Allies back from German home territory.

Dwight D. Eisenhower

Walter Model

Bernard Montgomery

Adolf Hitler

George S. Patton

BATTLE OF IWO JIMA (19TH FEB – 26TH MAR 1945)

Operation Detachment was one of the deadliest conflicts in US Marine Corps history. The Japanese death toll approached 21,000 soldiers. Some 7,000 US Marines were killed and 20,000 were wounded. For the United States, the victory at Iwo Jima, located 750 miles off the coast of Japan, provided the American Air Force with important airfields that would be used throughout the rest of the war in the Pacific.

Raymond A. Spruance

George Marshall

Emperor Hirohito

Franklin D. Roosevelt

Harold Henry Schultz

WHAT ELSE TO FIND

BATTLE OF THE ATLANTIC

1. Parachute flare
2. Signal lamp
3. Playing cards
4. Accordion
5. Fan
6. Smoking pipe
7. Shark
8. Enigma Machine
9. Toolbox
10. 6 Pairs of binoculars

03.09.193?

08.05.19

COLDITZ

1. Football
2. 5 rats
3. Tuba
4. Tobacco pipe
5. Saw
6. 2 Decoy soldiers
7. Bar of chocolate
8. Soldier escaping dressed as a woman
9. German shepherd dog
10. Hammer

193?

194?

DUNKIRK EVACUATION

1. Medical bag
2. Binoculars
3. Crab
4. 2 Water bottles (flasks)
5. Walking stick
6. Sandwich
7. Sand castle
8. Monocle
9. 3 Woollen blankets
10. Telescope

26.05.19?

04.06.19

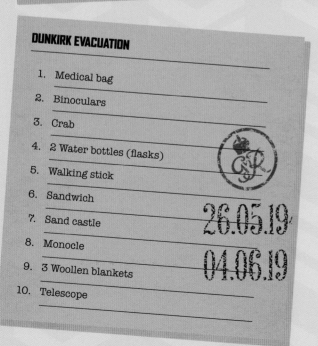

BATTLE OF BRITAIN

1. Green telephone
2. Fuel drum
3. Stove
4. Black lab
5. Radar screen
6. Spanner
7. Ammunition belt
8. Windsock
9. Church
10. Parachute

10.06.1940

?0.10.194?

THE BLITZ

SEP 1940

MAY 1941

1. 5 Black cats
2. Baby
3. Stethoscope
4. Milk bottles
5. Cup of tea
6. Torch
7. Whistle
8. 4 Stretchers
9. Postbox
10. 2 Prams

ATTACK ON PEARL HARBOR

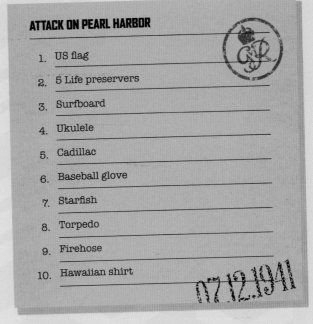

1. US flag
2. 5 Life preservers
3. Surfboard
4. Ukulele
5. Cadillac
6. Baseball glove
7. Starfish
8. Torpedo
9. Firehose
10. Hawaiian shirt

07.12.1941

BATTLE OF MIDWAY

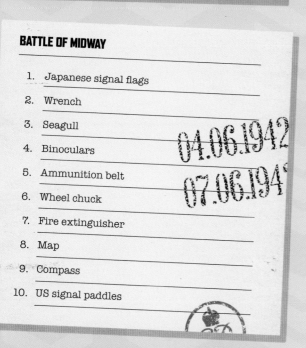

1. Japanese signal flags
2. Wrench
3. Seagull
4. Binoculars
5. Ammunition belt
6. Wheel chuck
7. Fire extinguisher
8. Map
9. Compass
10. US signal paddles

04.06.1942

07.06.194°

BATTLE OF STALINGRAD

1. Hammer and sickle
2. Megaphone
3. Bearded soldier
4. 5 Stone frogs
5. 2 Ammunition belts
6. Picture frame
7. Clock
8. Teddy
9. City map
10. Gas mask

23.08.1942

02.02.1943

BATTLE OF EL ALAMEIN

1. 4 Desert rats insignias
2. Lamp post
3. Beer bottle
4. Field telephone
5. Handkerchief
6. Kettle
7. 3 Foxes
8. Canned food
9. Bandage
10. 2 Cigarettes

23.10.1942

11.11.1942

BATTLE OF KURSK

1. Stretcher
2. Russian doll
3. Church
4. Hammer
5. Vodka bottle
6. Sickle
7. Map
8. Binoculars
9. 3 Pairs of goggles
10. Medical orderly

05.06.1943

23.08.1943

BATTLE OF MONTE CASSINO

1. Shop sign
2. 3 Radio operators
3. Map
4. Lizard
5. Bugle
6. Brown bear
7. Italian flag
8. Motorbike
9. Washing line
10. Spade

17.01.1944
18.05.1944

INVASION OF NORMANDY

1. 2 Para dummies "Ruperts"
2. Stick grenade
3. 7 Medical orderlies
4. 4 Radio operators
5. Life preserver
6. Bottle
7. Sweetheart photo
8. Red beret
9. Helmet with two bullet holes
10. Seasick soldier

06.06.1944

OPERATION MARKET GARDEN

1. Clog
2. Tulip
3. Dynamite
4. Road sign
5. Bicycle
6. Detonator plunger
7. RAF roundel
8. 2 Maps
9. Umbrella
10. Commandos

17.09.1944
25.09.1944

BATTLE OF THE BULGE

1. Sniper
2. Horse
3. Cigarette pack
4. Cup of Joe
5. Mortar team
6. Frag grenade
7. Snowman
8. Owl
9. Soup can
10. Tree

16.12.1944
25.01.1945

BATTLE OF IWO JIMA

1. Imperial Japanese flag
2. Sword
3. Map
4. Seagull
5. Cat
6. 2 Soldiers with flame throwers
7. Paper fan
8. Telescope
9. Surrendering soldier
10. Medical orderly

19.02.1945
26.03.1945